First World War
and Army of Occupation
War Diary
France, Belgium and Germany

57 DIVISION
Divisional Troops
Divisional Signal Company
1 September 1915 - 25 October 1915

WO95/2974/1

The Naval & Military Press Ltd
www.nmarchive.com
Published in association with The National Archives

Published by

The Naval & Military Press Ltd

Unit 10 Ridgewood Industrial Park,

Uckfield, East Sussex,

TN22 5QE England

Tel: +44 (0) 1825 749494

www.naval-military-press.com

www.nmarchive.com

This diary has been reprinted in facsimile from the original. Any imperfections are inevitably reproduced and the quality may fall short of modern type and cartographic standards.

© **Crown Copyright**
Images reproduced by permission of The National Archives, London, England, 2015.

Contents

Document type	Place/Title	Date From	Date To
Heading	WO95/2974-1		
Miscellaneous	Statement	31/08/1915	31/08/1915
Miscellaneous	Statement August 1st To 31st 1915	04/09/1915	04/09/1915
Heading	War Diary Of West Lancashire Divisional Signal Company, Royal Engineers. From 1st September. To 30th September.	01/10/1915	01/10/1915
War Diary	Canterbury.	01/09/1915	08/09/1915
War Diary	Bridge	13/09/1915	29/09/1915
Heading	War Diary And Statement from 1st to 30th September. 1915		
War Diary	Canterbury	08/09/1915	08/09/1915
War Diary	Wingham	22/09/1915	25/09/1915
Heading	War Diary Of 1/1st West Lancashire Divisional Signal Company Royal Engineers. From:- October 1st 1915 To:- October 31st 1915		
War Diary	Bridge	19/10/1915	27/10/1915
Heading	War Diary. Of 1/1st West Lancashire Divisional Signal Company Royal Engineers. From:- 1st November 1915. To:- 30th November 1915		
War Diary	Bridge	09/11/1915	24/11/1915
Heading	War Diary from 1st to 31st October. 1915. of 2/57th (West Lancs) Divisional Signal Co. R.E.		
War Diary	Wingham	12/10/1915	29/10/1915
Heading	War Diary Of 2/57th (West Lancs.) Divisional Signal Company, Royal Engineers. from 1st to 30th November 1915.		
War Diary	Wingham	10/10/1915	25/10/1915

wool / 254g (1)

wool / 254g / 274 (1)

S T A T E M E N T.

August 1st. to August 31st. 1916.

Unit:- 2/57th. (WEST LANCS.) DIV'L SIGNAL COMPANY R.E.

Division:- 57th. (WEST LANCS.) DIVISION.

Mobilization Centre:- St. Helens.

Station since occupied subsequent to concentration:- Old Park Camp, CANTERBURY.

Training:- This Unit is still attached to the 1/57th. Signal Company for training, but it has not been found necessary during the past month to obtain equipment from the 1/57th. Signal Company for training purposes, as the equipment of this Unit is practically complete, with the exception of Horses.

All the Officers of this Unit have attended Courses of Instruction in Signal Duties at a Signal Depot, and are qualified to instruct.

In view of the above facts, this Unit could, if necessary, be trained by its own Officers.

Discipline:- Good.

Administration:-
1. Medical Services...................Good.
2. Veterinary Services................Good.
3. Supply Services....................Good.
4. Ordnance Services..................Good.

Capt.

O/C 2/57 (West Lancs.) Div'l Signal Co. R.E.

S T A T E M E N T. AUGUST 1ST TO 31ST 1915.

Unit :- 1/1st West Lancashire Divisional Signal Company Royal Engineers.

Division :- 57th (West Lancashire) Division.

Mobilisation Centre :- ST-HELENS.

STATIONS since occupied subsequent to Concentration :- KNOWSLEY PARK; BESSELS GREEN; and CANTERBURY.

TRAINING :- Progressive Sectional and Combined Schemes have been carried out, in which the Reserve Signal Unit has taken part. Further Instructional Classes have been held for Royal Artillery Officers and for Infantry Officers. Also courses in Cable Laying for N.C.Os and men of the R.F.A..

The lack of Harness and Technical Stores has seriously limited the Training of the Unit and made the holding of Instructional Classes exceedingly difficult to carry out efficiently. Difficulty has still been experienced through the lack of an adequate number of Cable Wagons, Pack Saddlery, Harness, Telephones, and other Technical Equipment. Mobilization Stores are insufficient and inadequate for Units carrying on progressive training.

DISCIPLINE.:- Good.

ADMINISTRATION

1. MEDICAL SERVICES :- Good.

2. VETERINARY SERVICES :- Only fairly good.

3. SUPPLY SERVICES :- Very good.

4. ORDNANCE SERVICES :- Difficulty is still experienced in obtaining necessary Stores and Equipment.

SUPPLY OF REMOUNTS.;- The Unit is still short of its complement of horses. This is particularly felt in respect to deficiency in the proper stamp of light draught horses suitable for Cable Work.

W.Oppenheim
Major
O/C. WEST LANCS. DIV: SIGNAL CO. R.E.

TRAINING............ The 57th (W.L.) Divl Signal Coy R.E., in huts at the Old Park, continue training in Cable laying, visual signalling, station work, and combined schemes. Classes of Instruction as follows were held during the month and have just completed :-

Course of Instruction in Signalling

    6. 12 Artillery Officers.
    26 Infantry Officers.

Course of Instruction in Cable laying.

    12 Artillery N.C.Os.

The 2/1st W.L.D.Sig Coy R.E. are in huts at Old Park, and continue training in Cable Drill, Visual Signalling, Station Work, and combined Schemes. The want of Harness has been greatly felt as without this no practical cable laying could be carried out, but notice has now been received of an early delivery. The want of Horses is also greatly felt to allow this unit to get more advanced in its training. A number of horses have been received during the month but owing to Veterinary reasons had to be sent direct to the Veterinary Hospital.

The 2/1st Field Coy are still employed on Coast Defence Work between Whitstable and Ramsgate, leaving only a few Men at Wingham to complete their Engineer Training.

The 2/2nd Field Coy are fully engaged on Defence Works on the Military Canal, Winchelsea - Hythe.

The Provisional R.E. Company at Rye are completing the Rifle Range and on Coast Defences in that neighbourhood.

CONFIDENTIAL

WAR DIARY.

of

WEST LANCASHIRE DIVISIONAL SIGNAL COMPANY, ROYAL ENGINEERS.

FROM :- 1ST SEPTEMBER.

TO   :- 30TH SEPTEMBER.

HEADQUARTERS,
    BRIDGE,
    October 1915.

W.Oppenheim
——————————
         Major,
O/C. WEST LANCS. DIV. SIGNAL CO. R.E.

Army Form C. 2118.

WAR DIARY
~~INTELLIGENCE SUMMARY~~

(Erase heading not required.)

Instructions regarding War Diaries and Intelligence Summaries are contained in F.S. Regs., Part II and the Staff Manual respectively. Title pages will be prepared in manuscript.

Hour, Date, Place			Summary of Events and Information	Remarks and references to Appendices
1st September 1915.	CANTERBURY.		Detailed 4 men to attend course in Telephone Exchange Working at BISHOPS STORTFORD.	
6th	do	1915.	Commencement of Signalling Course for N.C.Os and men of the R.F.A. West Lancs Divn.	
6th	do	1915.	Commencement of Course of Instruction in Telephony and Signal Duties for N.C.Os of the South Eastern Mounted Brigade Signal Troop.	
8th	do	1915.	Change of Station from OLD PARK CAMP to BRIDGE under instructions from Divisional Headquarters.	
13th	do	1915. BRIDGE.	Detailed one Officer to attend Course in Signal Duties at BIGGLESWADE.	
14th	do	1915.	25 horses taken on strength from WINCHEAP Vet Hospital.	
19th	do	1915.	Lieut Browning attached for training returned for duty with LONDON QTC.	
20th	do	1915.	Commencement of Course of Instruction in Electricity and Telephony for Officers and N.C.Os of the South Eastern Mted Bde, Sussex Yeomanry, East Kent and West Kent Yeomanry Regts.	
29th	do	1915.	Detailed 4 men to attend Course of Telephone Exchange Working at BISHOPS STORTFORD.	

Eroppe
major

O/C. WEST LANCS. DIV. SIGNAL CO. R.E.

CONFIDENTIAL.

WAR DIARY AND STATEMENT

from 1st to 30th SEPTEMBER, 1915.

of

2/57th (WEST LANCS.) DIVISIONAL SIGNAL COMPANY, R.E.

Army Form C. 2118

WAR DIARY
or
INTELLIGENCE SUMMARY

(Erase heading not required.)

from 1st to 30th September, 1915.

Instructions regarding War Diaries and Intelligence Summaries are contained in F.S. Regs., Part II. and the Staff Manual respectively. Title Pages will be prepared in manuscript.

Place	Date	Hour	Summary of Events and Information	Remarks and references to Appendices
CANTERBURY.	8th	11-30 a.m.	Unit moved from Old Park Camp, CANTERBURY, into Billets at WINGHAM. Strength :- 6 Officers. 160 Other Ranks. 24 Horses. 5 Mules. 12 Wagons. 1 Cart.	
WINGHAM.	22nd		Lieut. F. Hayward was transferred to 1/57th (West Lancs.) Div'l Sig. Co., R.E. and was struck off the strength of this Unit accordingly.	
WINGHAM.	22nd		II Lieut. A.C. Hare was transferred to this Unit from 2/8th King's (Irish) Liverpool Regiment and taken on the strength of this Unit accordingly.	
WINGHAM.	25th	11-30 a.m.	Animals of this Unit inspected by Colonel Pratt, Remount Staff, War Office.	

1875. Wt. W593/826 1,000,000 4/15 J.B.C. & A. A.D.S.S./Forms/C. 2118.

C O N F I D E N T I A L.

W A R   D I A R Y

of

1/1ST WEST LANCASHIRE DIVISIONAL SIGNAL COMPANY ROYAL ENGINEERS.

FROM :- OCTOBER 1ST 1915

TO :- OCTOBER 31ST 1915.

[signature] Major,
O/C 1/1st West Lancashire Divisional Signal Co, R.E.

Headquarters,
BRIDGE,
Nr CANTERBURY.
November 1915.

Army Form C. 2118.

WAR DIARY
or
INTELLIGENCE SUMMARY.
(Erase heading not required.)

Instructions regarding War Diaries and Intelligence Summaries are contained in F. S. Regs., Part II. and the Staff Manual respectively. Title pages will be prepared in manuscript.

Hour, Date, Place		Summary of Events and Information	Remarks and references to Appendices
19/10/15.	BRIDGE.	Inspected DEAL and WALMER Coast Defence Telephone System.	
23/10/15.	do	19 mules received from Divisional Veterinary Hospital WINCHEAP, and taken on strength.	
24/10/15.	do	Lieutenant E.C. Glover proceeded overseas for service with the British Mediterranean Expeditionary Force.	
27/10/15.	do	Detailed an Officer and party to repair HAWKSHILL - WALMER - DEAL Coast Defence Telephone System for Commandant Royal Marine Depot, DEAL.	
27/10/15.	do	Detailed four men to attend a Course in Telephone Exchange Working at BISHOPS STORTFORD.	

Evoopeteum major

O/C 1/West Lancs. Div. Signal Co. R.E.

C O N F I D E N T I A L.

W A R   D I A R Y.

of

1/1ST WEST LANCASHIRE DIVISIONAL SIGNAL COMPANY ROYAL ENGINEERS.

FROM:- 1st November 1915.

TO:- 30th November 1915.

E. Oppenheim   Major,
O/C 1/1ST West Lancs Divl Signal Coy R.E.

Headquarters,
BRIDGE, KENT.
December 1915.

Army Form C. 2118.

WAR DIARY
or
INTELLIGENCE SUMMARY
(Erase heading not required.)

Instructions regarding War Diaries and Intelligence Summaries are contained in F.S. Regs., Part II. and the Staff Manual respectively. Title pages will be prepared in manuscript.

Hour, Date, Place		Summary of Events and Information	Remarks and references to Appendices
9/11/15.	BRIDGE.	Stocktaking of R.E. Stores on charge of Provisional R.E. Units, and Coast Defence Stores.	
10/11/15.	do	Inspection of Unit by Major-General Sandbach (Inspector of R.E. Units).	
17/11/15.	do	Inspection of First Line transport by the D.A.Q.M.G. 57th (West Lancs) Division.	
22/11/15.	do	Commencement of Instructional Course in Telephony and construction and repairing of instruments for N.C.Os and men of the Divisional Royal Artillery.	
22/11/15.	do	Inspected Coast Defence Telephone System HAWKSHILL - DEAL for reconstruction purposes.	
24/11/15.	do	Detailed Officer to report on Stores required for reerecting Coast Defence Telephone System at DEAL.	

EWoppwan Major
O/C. WEST LANCS. DIV. SIGNAL CO. R.E.

CONFIDENTIAL.

W A R   D I A R Y

from 1st to 31st OCTOBER, 1915.

- of -

2/57th (WEST LANCS.) DIVISIONAL SIGNAL CO., R.E.

Army Form C. 2118

WAR DIARY

~~INTELLIGENCE SUMMARY~~

(Erase heading not required.)

Instructions regarding War Diaries and Intelligence Summaries are contained in F. S. Regs., Part II. and the Staff Manual respectively. Title Pages will be prepared in manuscript.

From 1st to 31st October; 19 15.

Place	Date	Hour	Summary of Events and Information	Remarks and references to Appendices
WINGHAM.	12th	4 p.m.	Practice Alarm.	
WINGHAM.	15th	7 p.m.	Eleven men joined this Unit from the 3/57th (W.L.) Div'l Signal Company, R.E., WEETON.	
WINGHAM.	29th	10-45 p.m.	Practice Alarm.	

[signature] Capt.
O/C., 2/57th (W.L.) Div'l Signal Coy. R.E.

CONFIDENTIAL.

WAR DIARY

of

2/57th (WEST LANCS.) DIVISIONAL SIGNAL COMPANY, ROYAL ENGINEERS.

from 1st to 30th NOVEMBER, 1915.

Army Form C. 2118

WAR DIARY

~~INTELLIGENCE SUMMARY~~

(Erase heading not required.)

From 1st to 30th November, 1915.

Instructions regarding War Diaries and Intelligence Summaries are contained in F. S. Regs., Part II. and the Staff Manual respectively. Title Pages will be prepared in manuscript.

Place	Date	Hour	Summary of Events and Information	Remarks and references to Appendices
WINGHAM.	10th	11-30 a.m.	The Unit was inspected by Major General Sandbach, Inspector General Royal Engineers. In his Report to Headquarters, 2nd Army, Major General Sandbach expressed his satisfaction as to efficiency of the Unit.	
WINGHAM.	17th	3-45 p.m.	The D.A.Q.M.G. inspected the Transport of this Unit, on the CANTERBURY-WINGHAM ROAD. The D.A.Q.M.G. in his Report complained of Mules with Shoulder Galls; this has been remedied by special treatment of Breast Collars.	
WINGHAM.	25th	11-10 a.m.	Twelve Drivers were transferred to this Unit from the 3rd Line, and were taken on the strength of this Unit accordingly.	

L. Kent. Capt.
O/C., 2/57th (W.L.) Div'l Signal Company, R.E.

www.ingramcontent.com/pod-product-compliance
Lightning Source LLC
Chambersburg PA
CBHW081510160426
43193CB00014B/2644